Roll

A traditional rhyme

Illustrated by Ann Skelly

There were eight in the bed,
and the little one said...

Roll over, roll over.

So they all rolled over,
and one fell out.

So they all rolled over,
and one fell out.

There were six in the bed,
and the little one said...

Roll over, roll over.

6

So they all rolled over,
and one fell out.

There were five in the bed,
and the little one said...

Roll over, roll over.

So they all rolled over,
and one fell out.

There were four in the bed, and the little one said...

Roll over, roll over.

So they all rolled over,
and one fell out.

There were three in the bed,
and the little one said...

Roll over, roll over.

So they all rolled over,
and one fell out.

There were two in the bed,
and the little one said...

So they all rolled over,
and one fell out.

There was one in the bed,
and the little one said...

Good night!